# JURASSIC CLASSICS

# the PREHISTORIC MASTERS of LITERATURE

## VOLUME 1

*Written by Saskia Lacey* • *Illustrated by Sernur Isik*

# WELCOME TO JURASSIC CLASSICS

You're invited to discover the ancient tales dinosaurs once devoured millions of years ago, when the world was a fiercer, but no less literary, place. Jurassic Classics are stories that have been enjoyed by both cold-blooded and warm-blooded readers for eons. They include dinosaur dramas, prehistoric poems, and timeless fossils of fiction. Many of these masterpieces are still studied by scholars today, and they're sure to leave you hungry for more.

# WILLIAM SHAKESPEAREASAURUS

The Beastly Bard

## Let us begin with the leader of the literary herd, William Shakespeareasaurus!

A playwright, poet, and plant eater, Shakespeareasaurus' work roars with ferocious talent. All of his poems and plays are powerful creations—beings with beating hearts, teeth, and talons. Plays such as *The Tempest* and *A Midsummer Night's Dream* are like quick-footed, adventurous beasts, dashing this way and that, while tragic works like *Romeo and Juliet* and *Hamlet* howl with bitter anguish.

Having invented over 1,578 grunts, growls, and snorts, Shakespeareasaurus' talent for wordplay is unequaled. "Do you raise your snout at me?" and "It sets my teeth on edge" are just a few phrases this great author coined. Such wild wit cannot be contained to the prehistoric! Thankfully, years later, his writing is once again rising to its rightful place at the top of the literary pyramid.

### Sonnet for My Duck-Billed Damsel
#### By William Shakespeareasaurus

My damsel's eyes are nothing like the stars.
They do not sparkle, shimmer, or shine.
Her skin is not smooth, but blighted with scars.
Still, I adore her because she is mine.
For even a thousand flaws cannot cancel,
The love I have for my duck-billed damsel!

## THE KABLAMO THEATRE

Millions of years ago, the Kablamo Theatre was formed from the impact of a monstrous meteor. Rich or poor, carnivore or herbivore, dinosaurs of all species stampeded the theatre to watch the plays of Shakespeareasaurus.

*Romeo and Juliet*, Shakespeareasaurus' story of "star-crossed" lovers, was wildly popular throughout the prehistoric era. Its long run may be due to the fact that turf wars were a constant threat for all species. Many dinosaurs could relate to the Montague and Capulet herds battling over shared territory.

Of course, it is the love story of Romeo and Juliet that truly takes center stage. Dinosaurs were known to quote Shakespeareasaurus' words to each other during their courtships. Lines like "My heart's mate sprung from my herd's only hate" and "But soft! There squats my fairest maiden!" were fan favorites.

# Romeo & Juliet

BY WILLIAM SHAKESPEAREASAURUS

# Romeo & Juliet

### ROMEO
*A love-lorn ornithomimus
of the Montague pack*

### JULIET
*The fairest protoceratops
of the Capulet pack*

### THE HERD
*All-knowing dinosaurs
who narrate the plight of
Romeo and Juliet*

### MONTAGUES AND
### CAPULETS
*Two powerful dinosaur
families and longtime foes*

## ACT I

| | |
|---|---|
| THE HERD: | Two primitive packs, longsworn enemies, |
| | Have fiercely fought over land for centuries. |
| | But born from their beastly and bitter rage, |
| | Is the star-crossed love which lights our stage. |
| ROMEO: | Hark, what lady doth slurp from yonder pond? |
| | O, grisly goddess, thou art a grand sight. |
| | Never have I loved before this night. |
| | I offer my claw, my most noble miss. |
| | If thou art offended by its rough touch, |
| | May I present my snout for a tender kiss? |
| JULIET: | Good sir, you do wrong your claw too much. |
| | For claw to claw is like a kiss most polite. |
| ROMEO: | But have we not snouts to kiss with too? |
| JULIET: | Ay, sir, snouts we use for mannerly delights. |
| ROMEO: | O, then, my love, let snouts do what claws do. |
| JULIET: | Ay me, a Capulet has never been kissed so! |
| ROMEO: | Art thou a Capulet? Alas, no! |

## ACT II

| | |
|---|---|
| THE HERD: | At a secret meeting, Romeo and Juliet decide, |
| | Their forbidden love is one they must hide. |
| ROMEO: | But soft! There squats my fairest maiden! |
| | See how she slumps her cheek upon her claw? |
| | O, that I were a beetle upon that claw, |
| | I would make her charming cheek my haven. |
| JULIET: | O Romeo, my love burns for thee, |
| | Like the savage fire of the lava sea. |
| | How can my heart's true mate, |
| | Spring from my herd's only hate? |

ROMEO: Thy ferocious beauty gnaws at my heart.
Promise me that we shall never part.
Our warring families are a great threat.
Let us leave and be wed, my fair Juliet.

JULIET: My dear, honorable Romeo,
I will follow thee wherever thoust go.

ROMEO: O, rejoice, thy words have made my heart light!
Parting is such sweet sorrow, until tomorrow,
A thousand times goodnight!

## ACT III

| | |
|---|---|
| THE HERD: | But soon, the families learned of their plans, |
| | And forbid a happy union between the clans. |
| JULIET: | They can banish me, but not my devotion. |
| | My love for thee is as vast as the ocean. |
| | O, that I had wings to fly over this cruel cacti. |
| ROMEO: | I shall repair our most terrible grief, |
| | And destroy this poison wall, leaf by leaf. |
| JULIET: | Fair, Romeo, climb not for this is prickly ash. |
| | The cactus shall inspire the fiercest rash. |
| ROMEO: | I would rather suffer eternal itching, |
| | Than a day without thy sweet bewitching! |
| THE HERD: | Alas, no matter how the lovers tried, |
| | Neither dino could reach the other's side, |
| | For never was a story of more woe |
| | Than this of Juliet and her Romeo. |

# WILLIAM SHAKESPEARE

## 1594–1616

THE BARD OF AVON

**ONE HUNDRED AND FIFTY MILLION YEARS AFTER SHAKESPEAREASAURUS** wrote in the common prehistoric language *Roarassic*, William Shakespeare wrote in Early Modern English. Born to John Shakespeare and Mary Arden of Stratford-upon-Avon, today the playwright, poet, and actor is widely considered the finest author to ever write in English.

*"All the world's a stage,*
*And all the men and women merely players:*
*They have their exits and their entrances;*
*And one man in his time plays many parts."*
—As You Like It

Shakespeare was the third of six children. His father was a leather merchant and held positions as an alderman and bailiff, jobs similar to the work done by modern mayors. His mother was an heiress. Historians speculate that Shakespeare attended the King's New School, where he learned to read and write. As the child of a public official, he would have been able to attend for free.

In 1582, when he was 18, Shakespeare married Anne Hathaway, who was his senior by eight years. Together they had three children. He arrived in London in the late 1580s. By 1592, records show that Shakespeare was earning a living as an actor and playwright. Eventually, he became part-owner of a theater company called the King's Men, because their performances were so beloved by King James I.

A playwright and poet of enduring popularity, Shakespeare's works are still performed today—an impressive feat considering Shakespeare wrote them over 400 years ago. The bard penned romances, tragedies, and comedies. He even wrote tragicomedies, such as *The Winter's Tale* and *The Merchant of Venice*, which made audiences both laugh and cry. His playful and perceptive approach to language continues to inspire modern writers around the world. Shakespeare appears to have retired to Stratford around 1613, at age 49, where he died three years later.

## POPULAR WORKS

| Tragedies | Comedies | Histories |
|---|---|---|
| *Hamlet* | *A Midsummer Night's Dream* | *Henry IV, Part 1* |
| *Macbeth* | *Much Ado About Nothing* | *Henry IV, Part 2* |
| *Othello* | *Twelfth Night* | *Henry V* |
| *Romeo and Juliet* | *As You Like It* | *Richard II* |
| *Titus Andronicus* | *The Taming of the Shrew* | |
| | *The Merchant of Venice* | |

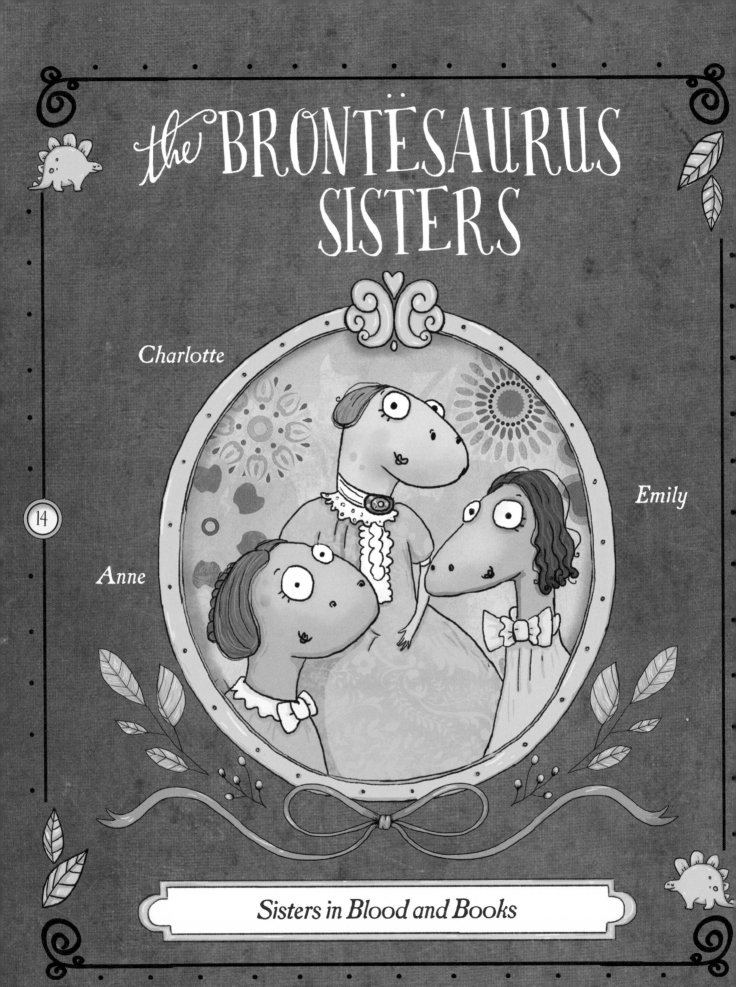

# the BRONTËSAURUS SISTERS

Charlotte

Anne

Emily

14

Sisters in Blood and Books

## It is with pleasure that we now turn our attention to

Emily Brontësaurus, the esteemed author of *Wuthering Heights*.

Unlike other writers of the age, Emily grew up far from the polite society of the big dinosaur herds. Her only sources of intellectual conversation were her sisters, Charlotte and Anne. Though many might find such isolation a bore, the sisters preferred their own quiet companionship.

Refined society held no charm for the Brontësaurus sisters. For in those primitive times, lady dinosaurs were expected to keep their claws clipped; float instead of stomp; and think only polite, well-mannered thoughts. They most certainly were not encouraged to write passionate tales of uncivilized love!

It was unusual that the sisters had literary ambitions, let alone pursued them. Charlotte, a small brontosaurus, was the only sister to become famous while she still walked the earth. Anne, the youngest of the three, adored writing odes to algae. Emily appeared to be shy and reserved, but her spirited nature is clearly seen in the fierce characters of *Wuthering Heights*.

The home of the Brontësaurus sisters and their family

Emily Brontësaurus' Pet

### A BOND FOR THE AGES

Emily Brontësaurus had a pet named Keeper—a devoted tree frog, who hopped beside her wherever she went. It is said that he mourned her death by following her coffin to the grave and croaking outside the cave for weeks.

 **THE BAD BOY**

Byron

Emily and Charlotte shared a fascination for a handsome dinosaur named Byron, a poet prone to long bouts of moping as well as the occasional carnivorous rampage. Strangely, the two sisters found such behavior delightfully attractive. Their love for Byron inspired the sisters to populate their novels with moody males.

Ah, doomed dinosaur love! Is there anything more tragic? After reading the tale of Catherine and Heathcliff, readers may feel as if their own hearts have been clawed to bits. Such is the power of Emily Brontësaurus' tortured prose.

Though *Wuthering Heights* is now a beloved classic, when it was published, reviewers described the book as "unfit for civilized beasts." Readers were offended by Catherine and Heathcliff's ferocious love, which roared against the rigid rules of society. Many dinosaurs wished to have the book banned. It wasn't until many years later that the genius of *Wuthering Heights* was truly recognized.

### Ode to Algae
By Anne Brontësaurus

Oh my dearest green slime,
You warm this heart of mine.
While others may scream, "Yuck!"
I adore your magnificent muck.

# Wuthering Heights

## BY EMILY BRONTËSAURUS

# Wuthering Heights

**CATHERINE**
*A spoiled brontosaurus driven mad by her heart's desire*

**HEATHCLIFF**
*A handsome velociraptor with a dark soul*

**EDGAR**
*A proper Jurassic gentleman*

**ISABELLA**
*Edgar's long-necked, silly sister*

If one hopes to read a happy love story, it is best to look elsewhere. What follows is the tragic tale of Catherine and Heathcliff.

In upbringing, no two dinosaurs were ever more different. Catherine, a beautiful brontosaurus, lived in a grand mansion made of bones and boulders. While Heathcliff, a brooding velociraptor, had no lair to call his own. Still, in their hearts, the two beastly creatures were very much alike.

They lived by Wuthering Heights—a glorious tar pit brimming with the muddiest muck and the gloopiest gunk. Catherine and Heathcliff loved nothing better than to spend whole days seeking out trouble, crashing and bashing through the swamplands.

"Heathcliff is me, and I am him," Catherine howled. "Our hearts will be joined forever in the muck of the swamp!" Both dinosaurs were sure nothing could tear them apart. Sadly that was not to be their fate.

One day, while Catherine and Heathcliff were frolicking among the swamp lilies, they came upon a proper pair of brontosauri.

"How do you do?" twittered the lady reptile. "My name is Isabella Linton, and this is my dear brother, Edgar."

Upon seeing Catherine, Edgar's tail trembled, "Who is this dazzling dinosauress?"

"She's mine!" Heathcliff growled.

"What a claim," Edgar gasped. "Isabella, don't get too close to this lowly beast, he'll likely ruin your finery with his filthy claws."

Heathcliff roared and took a swipe at Edgar.

"Oh Heathcliff, do calm down," Catherine murmured. Then, she turned to Edgar and Isabella. "My name is Catherine. It's a pleasure to meet such refined company."

Overcome by her beauty, it was not long before Edgar swooned, "Marry me!"

It was all too much for Heathcliff. He turned toward Catherine and bared his teeth. "You cannot have us both. Choose me—nay your soul!—and we will spend our days running wild in Wuthering Heights."

Catherine tortured herself comparing the two suitors. Edgar was handsome, a true gentleman—unlike Heathcliff, who spoke only in grumbles and growls. But oh, how fiercely he growled!

"Choose me and the sun will shine brighter because of our perfect love!" Edgar begged.

"This ninny couldn't love you as much in an eon as I could in a day," Heathcliff roared.

To the surprise of everyone, Isabella waded into the swamp and confessed her own love for the moody velociraptor.

"Away from me!" The raptor pushed Isabella into the tar, and her brother raced in after her. Heathcliff had a black heart that beat for only one dinosaur—Catherine.

"You have driven me to madness," Catherine wailed.

"My heart's darling!" Heathcliff tried to lunge forward, but his feet were held fast by the sticky muck.

Poor Isabella and Edgar could only moan as they sank deeper and deeper into the tar pits. Trapped by the gloomy gloop they held so dear, Catherine and Heathcliff could not escape their doomed love, nor the sticky depths of Wuthering Heights.

# EMILY BRONTË

## JULY 30, 1818–DECEMBER 19, 1848

A WILD AND SPIRITED TALENT

**EMILY JANE BRONTË WAS AN ENGLISH NOVELIST WHOSE IMAGINATION** was as wild as the moors she loved. Although she published less than 200 years ago, Emily left behind little for scholars to study, and her life remains nearly as mysterious as her brontosaurus counterparts.

> *"She burned too bright for this world."*
> —Wuthering Heights

Emily's early life was marked by tragedy. Her mother and two sisters died while she was still young. She spent her days with her remaining family, including her father, sisters Charlotte and Anne, and their brother Branwell. They amused themselves by exploring the moors, creating elaborate games, and writing.

Like other women who dared to write at that time, the Brontë sisters struggled to find someone who would publish their work. They refused to give up and eventually published their work under male pen names. The first of these works, *Poems by Currer, Ellis and Acton Bell,* cost the Brontës nearly £50 to produce and sold just two miserable copies. It contained more than 20 poems and revealed Emily's genius, although critics would not admire her work until many years later. As Ellis Bell, Emily was able to publish her novel, *Wuthering Heights*. While the book is now known as a literary classic, respected for its raw emotion and fearless originality, it was considered a failure when it was first released.

Except for a few brief periods, Emily spent most of her life at home. In 1835, Charlotte obtained a position teaching. Emily accompanied Charlotte as a pupil, but was so homesick that she left after only three months. Three years later, Emily spent six months teaching before resigning. In 1842, Charlotte and Emily, planning to start a school for girls, traveled to Brussels to study school management and foreign languages; however, the death of their aunt Elizabeth forced them to return home shortly after. At just 30 years old, Emily died of what scholars believe to be tuberculosis. A common, but sad, end for an uncommon woman who secured her legacy as a brave and creative writer with just a single novel and a collection of poems.

## A SINGULAR MASTERPIECE

*Wuthering Heights*

# EDGAR ALLAN TERRORDACTYL

*The World's First Goth*

# Edgar Allan Terrordactyl used his literary talents

to write peculiar poems, spooky short stories, and a nightmarish novel.

Descriptions of Edgar Allan Terrordactyl's physical appearance are numerous. Many ancient scholars spoke of the author's dark, hypnotic eyes and unruly hair, which was "the color of the midnight sky." Such accounts make the author sound like a creature from one of his own tales of terror.

Edgar Allan Terrordactyl's life was not an easy one. His parents died when he was just a hatchling. After their death, the young dinosaur was taken under the wings of a wealthy pair of pterodactyls, but he did not fit in with his new family's nest. Even after achieving literary fame, the author struggled to feed himself and was often reduced to scavenging.

Still, Terrordactyl always found solace soaring above the treetops. The author delighted in swooping down on unsuspecting jungle creatures and dreamt up his scariest stories during long flights.

*Edgar Allan Terrordactyl swooping down on unsuspecting jungle creatures*

## CRUNCHING THE CODE

Edgar Allan Terrordactyl was devoted to secret codes. In his day, dinosaurs would build secret messages using sticks, stones, bones, and leaves. Terrordactyl was famous for solving codes simply by eating them. His short story, *The Gold-Bug,* featured a character who must solve a leaf-and-stick code in order to find buried treasure.

Themes of tragedy and beauty were often intertwined in Terrordactyl's writing. *The Raven* remains the author's most famous work and one of the most well-known poems of all time. Its magic lies in the deep connection between the poem's setting—a gloomy cave—and its main character, a mourning stegosaurus. The dark setting highlights the struggles of its main character. Dinosaur herds of all species celebrated Terrordactyl as a master of melancholy.

## WHODUNNIT? HEDUNNIT!

A dark and strange mind such as Terrordactyl's was destined to stretch the boundaries of fiction. It was the author's love of thrills and chills that led him to create a new type of tale— the detective story. *The Murders in the Rue Morgue,* a short story about a dinosaur who solves two mysterious murders, would inspire all detective tales to come, including Sir Arthur Conandactyl's Sherlock Holmes stories.

# The Raven

## BY EDGAR ALLAN TERRORDACTYL

# The Raven

**THE LONELY STEGOSAURUS**
*A melancholy dinosaur mourning his lost love*

**THE RAVEN**
*The stegosaurus' enigmatic and wise visitor*

Once upon a midnight moody,
While I sat alone, sad and broody,
I thought about my lost love,
The gruesome beauty I adore
The one I call, "Vile Valentine,"
The one who owns this heart of mine.
She is my deadly darling,
My exquisite eyesore,
My grumpy, lumpy love—
That fair Stegosaurus named Lenore.

I thought of her and nothing more.

Then, outside I heard a rapping,
The most obnoxious tap-tapping,

What sort of rude beast would dare,
To bother me in my lair?
I had hoped to mope in private,
And so tried hard to ignore
The tap-tapping, the endless,
Exasperating rapping at my door.

Give me silence and nothing more!

Suddenly, a thing with feathers,
On the wings of wild and stormy weather,
Crashed through my cave's stately décor.
I watched as he thrashed my haven,
A bird black as night—a raven.
"Let me grieve in peace," I said with a roar.

The raven simply said, "Nevermore."

The bird had the strange nobility
Of those with secret ability.
Might he possess a magic
That could help me find Lenore?
I clenched each claw and tried
To put aside my silly pride,
"When shall I see my lethal love,
The Stegosaurus that I adore?"

The bird said again, "Nevermore."

The same response—a most cruel trick,
Surely meant to tease the heartsick!
Why must he keep repeating, "Nevermore?"
Ah! I see, this is a game—
All his answers shall be the same.

I must ask a different question;
This time I shall be pleased, unlike before.
"Dear Raven, will my sad days continue?"
I asked with a rumbling roar.

The raven smiled and said, "Evermore."

The game had become absurd;
The bird now spoke different words?
I began to wail and feeling my heart start to fail,
I knew then, that I would never see again,
My beautiful bonehead, my exquisite eyesore,
My shabby, crabby sweetie, my Lenore.

I whispered quietly, "Nevermore."

# EDGAR ALLAN POE

## January 19, 1809–October 7, 1849

MASTER OF THE LITERARY DARK ARTS

**Like his kindred pterodactyl spirit, American writer Edgar Allan Poe** wrote countless poems and short stories, inventing entire genres of literature. He was also an editor and critic, and millions of years after his Jurassic brother roamed the literary landscape, he discovered new depths to the art of melancholy.

> *"I became insane, with long intervals of horrible sanity."*
> —A Letter from Poe to a Reader

Poe's life was not an easy one. Born to traveling actors, he was orphaned at just three years old when his parents died and raised by a wealthy tobacco merchant. His guardian did little to fund his future, and in 1826, when Poe attended the University of Virgina, he was forced to drop out because he lacked the funds to pay. Poe returned home to find his fiancée, Elmira Royster, had become engaged to somebody else. Heartbroken, Poe left home again.

The next year, Poe published his first book, *Tamerlane and Other Poems*, and joined the army. He was accepted to West Point, a military academy, where he excelled academically, but was kicked out after a year for neglecting his duties.

Following his passion, Poe began to write full time. He moved to Baltimore, where he lived with his aunt and her daughter, Virginia, who became both Poe's wife and muse. Poe landed a position as an editor at a magazine called the *Southern Literary Messenger*, where he gained a reputation as a scathing critic and sensational storyteller. Over the next decade, he sought adventure and work in New York City, where he penned his first and only novel, and in Philadelphia where he wrote for a number of magazines.

Today, Poe is considered a literary genius who invented entire genres. Modern mysteries, horror stories, and science fiction all owe great debts to his pioneering work. Despite his fame, Poe was barely able to support himself for most of his lifetime. His beloved wife, Virginia, died in 1847. Poe himself died just two years later; his last words were "Lord, help my poor soul."

## POPULAR WORKS

*Annabel Lee*
*The Narrative of Arthur Gordon Pym of Nantucket*
*The Fall of the House of Usher*
*The Murders in the Rue Morgue*
*The Tell-Tale Heart*

This library edition published in 2018 by Walter Foster Jr.,
an imprint of The Quarto Group
6 Orchard Road, Suite 100
Lake Forest, CA 92630

Written by Saskia Lacey
Edited by Heidi Fiedler
Illustrated by Sernur Isik

Distributed in the United States and Canada by
Lerner Publisher Services
241 First Avenue North
Minneapolis, MN 55401 U.S.A.
www.lernerbooks.com

First Library Edition

Library of Congress Cataloging-in-Publication Data

Names: Lacey, Saskia, author. | Isik, Sernur, illustrator.
Title: The prehistoric masters of literature / written by Saskia Lacey ;
    illustrated by Sernur Isik.
Description: Lake Forest, CA : Quarto Group, [2017] | Series: Jurassic
    classics | Summary: "Famous literary figures are given dinosaur-inspired
    pseudonyms and prehistoric biographies as a way of introducing young
    readers to classic literature"-- Provided by publisher. Contents: Volume
    1: William Shakespeareasaurus -- The Brontesaurus sisters -- Edgar Allan
    Terrordactyl. Contents: Volume 2: Mark Twainceratops -- Charles
    Dickensodocus -- Jane Austenlovenator.
Identifiers: LCCN 2017035002| ISBN 9781942875550 (v. 1 : hardcover) | ISBN
    9781942875567 (v. 2 : hardcover)
Subjects: LCSH: Canon (Literature)--Parodies, imitations, etc.--Juvenile
    literature. | Authors--Biography--Juvenile literature. | Shakespeare,
    William, 1564-1616--Juvenile literature. | Brontë, Anne,
    1820-1849--Juvenile literature. | Brontë, Charlotte, 1816-1855--Juvenile
    literature. | Brontë, Emily, 1818-1848--Juvenile literature. | Poe, Edgar
    Allan, 1809-1849--Juvenile literature. | Twain, Mark, 1835-1910--Juvenile
    literature. | Dickens, Charles, 1812-1870--Juvenile literature. | Austen,
    Jane, 1775-1817--Juvenile literature. | CYAC: Humorous stories. |
    Dinosaurs--Fiction. | Authors--Fiction.
Classification: LCC PZ7.1.L2 Pr 2017 | DDC [Fic]--dc23
LC record available at https://lccn.loc.gov/2017035002

Printed in USA
9 8 7 6 5 4 3 2 1